COME HERE!

Teach Your Dog to Come When Called

Carol Miller

First Printing, 2013

Printed in the United States of America

Liability Disclaimer

By reading this document, you assume all risks associated with using the advice given below, with a full understanding that you, solely, are responsible for anything that may occur as a result of putting this information into action in any way, and regardless of your interpretation of the advice.

This book is intended for educational purposes only and does not replace a consultation with a certified animal behaviorist, veterinarian, or other qualified animal professional.

COME HERE!

Teach Your Dog to Come When Called

Table of Contents

Introduction

Of all the things you can train your dog to do, coming when called, or "recalling" as we dog trainers call it, is by far the most important. This command can literally save your dog's life. But as important as it is, it is also one of the most difficult things to teach reliably. Yes, you probably know someone who has a dog who always comes when they call, but they have either worked on this for a long time or have a dog who by nature wants to stay near their owner. This can come about a number of ways, but for the rest of us, we need to train it, and train it very well.

If your dog does the "I'll be over there in a minute!" type of recall, this guide will teach you how to turn that into "Sure, right away!". If your dog loves freedom and takes off the moment he's loose, you'll be learning how to make him care more that you're with him, and to choose to come back to you when you call. If your dog chases squirrels and other dogs, you'll see how to teach him to ignore distractions in favor of coming to you.

A note about expectations: It's a fact that some dogs are easier to teach a recall to than others. And with any dog, there are different levels of performance that you have to teach through.

Keep in mind that just because your dog always comes to you in the house or backyard, when off leash in the woods, he almost certainly will take off and explore unless you have taught him "college" level recall skills.

A Quick Look at Training Basics

This book assumes you have done at least some rudimentary training with your dog, such as "Sit", "Down" and basic attention skills. If not, consider starting with one of my other books, either "Six Weeks to a Better Behaved Puppy" or "Dog Training: A Professional Trainer Shares Her Secrets" to get some foundation skills before attempting to teach a great recall. Recalling is a more advanced behavior, and you'll find your results will be much better if your dog already pays at least SOME attention to you before you embark on this journey.

This training plan is based on Positive Reinforcement Choice-Based Training, which means no force is used at all. "Choice-Based" means that we look for the dog to make the right choice, allowing for the possibility of wrong choices. If the dog chooses correctly (how we want him to), he is rewarded. If he makes a poor choice, he doesn't get a reward, and we try again to explain to him what we want. If you look at training as school for your dog, you'll see that you don't need to scold or punish him. We just try harder to get him to understand and want to do it.

Training Levels

I like to look at your dog's abilities as having three levels: "Kinda got it", "Got it when nothing exciting is happening", and "Got it no matter what".

"Kinda got it" is where I find most dogs are at in most of their education. Most of the time, they try to do what you ask, but they aren't really good at it. Many times they are just taking their best guess and hoping to get a treat for it. This is very obvious when your dog starts doing everything you've taught them one after another, hoping something will be what you want enough to give them a reward.

"Got it when nothing exciting is happening" is common for things like "Sit". Your dog will sit almost any time you ask, unless company walks in the door, he's playing with another dog, or doing pretty much anything interesting to him. But when things are calm and easy, he has no problem responding quickly.

"Got it no matter what" is like college level per-formance for dogs. He responds quickly and correctly to what you ask, no matter if the door-bell just rang, he's meeting a stranger, or he's playing in the dog park. He knows what you want and he ignores distractions. Very few dog owners take their dog to this level of obedience. It re-quires consistent effort and a good training plan.

This book gives you a good training plan. The consistent effort needed to train a fabulous recall is up to you.

Other Things Covered in This Program

Since a fabulous recall requires a fabulous ability to ignore the lure of outside distractions, this program includes other behaviors that will work hand-in-hand with your recall training in order to accomplish that. These are:

- **Sit.** A fast, reflexive response to the "Sit" command will help your dog learn to listen to you more effectively.

- **Down.** You will be teaching an "Emergen-cy Down" to your dog. Sometimes calling your dog is the wrong thing to do – say your dog is across the street, and a car is coming down the road. You can't call him without risking him getting hit. If you do nothing, he may decide to come back to you at the wrong moment. If you can tell him to lie down and stay, you can freeze him in place until it's safe for him to come to you. That's what we will be working toward during this program.

- **Leave It.** Almost everything has an element of "Leave It" in it. Nice leash walking – ignore that dog, don't pull toward that bush. Come when I call – ignore that smell, don't follow that person. "Leave It" teaches your dog not to need to go after things just because they are there, a critical skill.

- **Stay.** I love stays, because they help your dog relax when things are going on. The ability to remain under control even though someone runs past, drops food on the floor or throws his favorite toy, helps tremendously with being able to come when called no matter what.

- **Polite Leash Walking.** If your dog can't walk with you on the leash without trying to pull you to things, how is he going to come when you call him if he isn't on leash? He simply must learn to be outside without having to rush to anything he feels like (unless you've told him it's okay).

How to Use This Training Plan

Broken into "Weeks", this is a six-step training plan. Please take this as a general structure, not a fixed schedule. You simply must work at your dog's pace if you are to accomplish anything with him. If he's not ready to move ahead, don't. Stay at the level you are on until your dog can meet the requirements to move on. Each lesson will have a checklist to help you determine whether it's time to move ahead.

The most important thing you can do is build a strong foundation. If you move too quickly, your dog's performance will get worse and worse as his understanding of what you want gets weaker. Be sure he "gets" it before moving on.

Okay, enough preliminaries. Let's get started...

Week One

Things to accomplish:

- Understand the value of different reinforcers (rewards)
- Make a list of possible reinforcers with their relative value to your dog
- Understand the influence of distractions
- Make a list of possible distractions and their relative difficulty for your dog
- Work on foundation "Sit" and "Down"
- Practice the "Collar Grab"
- Work on foundation recalls
- Work on foundation "Leave It"
- Work on foundation leash walking
- Work on foundation "Stay"

The Keys to Creating a Terrific Recall

A terrific recall can save your dog's life. It allows the possibility of freedom from restraint in locations where this is permitted, such as some beaches, parks and trails. It makes taking your dog out a pleasure rather than a struggle.

In order to have a terrific recall, you must begin to understand the various reasons why a dog may choose not to come to you. Most dogs have an "In a minute!" type recall – they want to finish what they're doing, and then they'll come. This is simply not good enough. If we call our dog, we need him to respond promptly and enthusiastically. Here are some reasons that this may be difficult to achieve:

- **His breed** – some breeds have been specifically created for independent work, or to follow a scent no matter what.
- **His temperament** – while some dogs are what we call "Velcro" dogs, sticking to their owners at all times, many dogs are more secure and adventurous, and love exploring the environment.
- **His training** – some lucky people have dogs that just love to do what they say, but the rest of us must train our dogs, and train thoroughly around the things that call to him the most.

Before we can start, we must understand two critical elements of all training – the power of reinforcers, or rewards, and the influence of distractions.

A reinforcer is anything that your dog likes. This includes things that you do for or with him, such as food, treats, toys, games, belly rubs, or massages, and also includes things that you don't necessarily have anything to do with, such as great smells in the grass, other animals around while on a walk, people walking past a window, garbage on the ground, and any of dozens, even hundreds of other things that your dog is pulled to.

A distraction is exactly what it sounds like – something that takes your dog's focus away from what he is doing. Reinforcers are usually distractions as well – chasing a squirrel may be a reinforcer, while seeing a squirrel during a walk would be a distraction.

The laws of learning state that "Reinforcement builds behavior." This works both for and against us. When we reinforce our dog with food or a great game after he does something we like, we increase the chance that it will happen again. The downside is that when your dog eats something great off of your counter, this is also a reinforcer, and the chance that he will check the counter again is greatly increased.

The same holds true for recalls. If you constantly reward your dog for coming to you, he will do it more. If instead, being free means the fun game of chasing squirrels, he will choose the squirrels.

All of this means we must work hard to be the source of the dog's reinforcement, and minimize his chances of being rewarded by his environment.

In this course, we will focus not only on recalling, but also on building an "Emergency Down", better leash walking, stronger stays, and a fantastic "Leave It". These skills all tie into building a terrific recall for your dog by increasing his attention on you and his ability to ignore distractions.

NOTE: This first week may be very easy for you and your dog, but it is essential to tighten up his foundational skills to a high level if you expect a great recall. I can't stress enough the importance of working consistently every day on these simple exercises. You are setting the stage for success here, and even if the exercises seem too easy for your dog, he will get great value from the strengthening you will be doing this week.

CRITICAL POINT!!! During the early stages of training, you must NEVER call your dog unless you are 100% certain that he will come to you! Never call him for things he doesn't like, like a bath or toenail trim, or going inside if he would rather stay out. Go and get him if you aren't positive he will come.

Training Progression

Below describes the way you should structure your work during your dog training. You want to balance setting your dog up for success with providing enough challenge that he can stretch his abilities. This means that occasionally he will make a wrong choice, but if you follow the process laid out below, you will help him learn by making choices without going far beyond his ability to perform correctly.

Your dog learns to want to make the right choice since you are reinforcing him for his right decision. He always has a choice, since you can't make him do the right thing. Given that from the early stages of training you have been making it easy for him to be right, he will continue to make good choices as the challenges increase.

There are three main stages of your training plan (these go along with the stages of learning discussed earlier).

BEGINNING: At this stage, we set up our training exercises to be extremely easy for your dog. You want him to have a very good chance of being right, which helps him to understand what it is that you are trying to get him to do. By controlling what happens and making his correct choices very enticing, you make is easy to be right and very difficult to make a wrong choice.

19

INTERMEDIATE: As your dog gets an understanding of what you want from him, you begin to allow him to have more choices available. You are still making it fairly easy to make the right choice, but now there are more opportunities to be distracted. Since you have worked long enough on his Beginning Level exercises, he shouldn't find it too hard to make the correct choice among many.

PROOFING: After much practice in various Intermediate Level exercises and environments, it's time to check to see if his understanding and desire can withstand extremely difficult situations. By making it easy for him to choose wrongly and difficult to be right, you will see if your dog can handle most real-life situations. Since you have practiced so much in the Middle level, your dog should be able to handle almost anything you can throw at him.

You will need to continue to work on recalls for the life of your dog, practicing here and there, as well as proofing occasionally just to be sure your dog is still able to perform correctly no matter what.

That said, there are some dogs that will never be 100% safe off leash. If you can see that your dog will not choose to come to you at all times, be safe and keep him on a long line. Maybe with more training you can see better results, but until then, safety first. But even a 70% recall might save his life if your dog slips out the door one day. Keep working on it so it will be there when you need it!

THINGS TO DO THIS WEEK

First Day: Make a list of your dog's reinforcers and rank them.

List all of the things your dog likes, even if they aren't things you give him (e.g. chasing squirrels). After you've listed everything you can think of, put a letter "A", "B" or "C" by each thing, "C" meaning it has little value to your dog, "A" meaning he would pretty much do anything for it. Once you have your list, copy it to the bonus printable sheet in ranking order from "A" to "C", as you'll need to refer to this list during training. Here are some suggestions as a starting point: steak, chicken, salami, cheese, his kibble, game of tug, toss a ball, throw a frisbee, get a belly rub, go for a ride in the car.

First Day: Make a list of your dog's distractions and rank them.

List all of the things that challenge your dog. Many of the items on your reinforcers list are tremendous distractions for your dog as well (imagine your dog running past a bowl of food on his way to you). After you've listed everything you can think of, put a number 1 through 10 by each thing, 1 meaning it has little difficulty for your dog, 10 meaning it's a super difficult challenge. Once you have your list, copy it to the bonus printable sheet in ranking order from 10 down to 1, as you'll be referring to this list while you're training your dog. Here are some suggestions to get you started: squirrels, deer, geese, other dogs, people, food on the ground, great smell, rabbit poop, sign posts, mailbox posts, toys, shoes on the floor.

Each Day: Practice the "Sit" exercise with a release (Implied "Stay"). "C" value treats.

Practice asking your dog to "Sit". Be sure to reward your dog each time, saying "Yes!" immediately as his bottom touches the floor, then give him a treat. Quickly say "Okay" and move to release him from the sit. Be sure to remember that "Sit" has a beginning AND an end. Do this in a place that is quiet and has no distractions to help set him up for success. Remember, if you can't reward him for doing it right, he isn't learning anything. As the week progresses, begin to wait longer before saying "Okay" and moving to release him.

Each Day: Practice the "Down" exercise with a release (Implied "Stay"). "C" value treats.

Same as "Sit" only with a "Down" instead.

Each Day: Play the "Collar Grab" game. "C" value treats.

Sit your dog in front of you, and have a treat hidden in one hand. Reach for his collar (at the side of his body, not over his head) with your free hand. Take it gently, and while holding it, give him the treat with your other hand. Let go. Repeat 4 or 5 times in a session. If your dog is hand shy or nervous about this, start by just moving your hand by the side of his face, then give the treat. Gradually work up to reaching to just touch the collar, then gently holding it.

You should use a collar grab every time you do a recall with your dog. It is important to be able to grab your dog when you need to, and this game also helps nervous dogs get used to hands coming at them.

Each Day: Practice simple recalls to improve your dog's focus on you. "B" value treats.

Step 1: Say "Yes!" and treat for voluntary eye contact (you don't do anything, he just looked at you).

Step 2: Say his name, and when he looks at you, say "Yes!" and treat.

Step 3: Say his name and take a few steps back, say "Yes!" when he turns toward you, CG (grab his collar) and treat when he arrives.

Step 4: Say his name when he is slightly distracted, and when he looks at you, say "Yes!", CG and treat when he arrives.

Step 5: Begin to say his cue ("Buddy, Here!") when he is near you, and when he looks at you, CG and say "Yes!" and treat.

Step 6: Say his cue and take a few steps back, say "Yes!" when he turns toward you, CG and treat when he arrives.

Step 7: Say his cue when he is slightly distracted, and when he looks at you, say "Yes!", CG and treat when he arrives.

Step 8: Do this in different locations both in the house and outside.

KEEP YOUR RECALLS TO A SHORT DISTANCE AT THIS POINT AND ONLY CALL IF YOU

KNOW HE WILL COME! NO TRYING BIG CHALLENGES THIS WEEK!!!!

Each Day: Work on Beginning Leash Manners. "B" value treats.

Exercise 1: Have high level treats in your hand. For just a few minutes several times a day, put your dog on a regular leash (not a retractable leash) in your kitchen, bathroom, basement, or other place with very few distractions around. Don't go anywhere – just stand still and every time your dog looks at you, say "Yes!" and give him a treat. Your goal is to begin to have your dog feel that you matter when he is on leash – to most dogs the owner is simply a dead weight to be pulled around. With this exercise you are beginning to show the dog that paying attention to you has value to him while he is leashed.

Exercise 2, first couple of days: With your dog off leash inside the house, put your dog in a sit. Move yourself so that he is on your side, sitting facing the same direction as you are. Say "Yes!" and give him a treat every second or so for a short while to get him to begin to build a "Reinforcement Zone", or sticky spot, on your side. The more he feels that's a great place to be, the easier it will be to teach him to walk nicely at your side. Repeat this exercise for just a minute or so a couple of times a day, if possible. If he gets up, don't worry about it, just start over. If you can't keep him there, you might need to use better treats for a bit until he begins to stay with you more.

Exercise 2, rest of the week: With your dog off leash inside the house, move into the sitting position described in Exercise 2 above, your new "Reinforcement Zone". Say "Yes!" and treat your dog a couple of times in this position. Then say "Okay" and take one large step forward. If your dog follows you, treat him just as he arrives next to your leg. If he doesn't follow, pat your leg, make noises, etc. to encourage him to move toward you, and then treat when he arrives. Work toward moving around the house with your dog moving into position with you. By the end of the week, you hopefully will have him walking nicely next to your side for at least 10 feet or so. Start slowly, just a step at a time, and work up to several steps before treating.

If your dog wanders off, don't acknowledge it, just keep moving away from him, and he may join you again. If not, try again in a bit with better treats or when he is more hungry. If he continues to leave you, go back to the first stage of this exercise and build your "Reinforcement Zone" more strongly. Remember never to say "No" or reprimand him for leaving you. This is an "error-less" exercise – we just build the good behavior up while ignoring any unwanted behaviors.

Each Day: Work on Impulse Control with the "Leave It" game. "C" treats.

Leave It Game Stage One: With low value treats, such as his kibbles, in one hand and your dog sitting in front of you, say "Leave It" and then offer your treat hand to your dog. As he grabs for the treats, close your hand quickly, being sure he does not get a treat. Let him sniff, lick, paw, nibble and even bite at your hand – don't move at all, don't say anything. Wait until he stops trying to get at the food out of frustration, then quickly open your hand and give him another chance at it. Go through the process again until he gives up, then open your hand again. When he finally figures out that trying to take a treat won't get him one and he doesn't move at it, pick a treat up with your other hand and feed it to him. If he tries for the treats again, repeat the process. Keep this up until you can feed him the treats one at a time without him trying to get them himself. Be sure to only say the cue once, at the beginning of the exercise.

CRITICAL TIP: DOG NEVER GETS TO WIN BY GRABBING.

Each Day: Work on "Sit-Stay". "B" value treats.

Stage 1, for two days: There are three factors in the "Stay" command – distance (how far you get from the dog), duration (how long your dog can hold a stay) and distractions (things going on around him – this is the hardest factor). This week, work only on the easiest stays, short distance and duration with no distractions. Next week you will begin to add to the difficulty, but only one factor at a time. From in front of your dog, ask him to sit, then hold your hand out like a traffic signal and quietly say "Stay". Look at him for a second, then lean forward and give him a treat. Be sure to quickly reach it all the way to him so he doesn't get up to get it. Stand back up straight, and then say, "Okay" quietly and move to indicate the dog can move around now. Don't make a big deal of the release – you don't want it to be more fun than the stay.

Don't be tempted to make it harder yet – build a strong foundation first. Begin to do 3-4 of these stays in a row before releasing your dog, so that he begins to relax into the stay and doesn't look forward to the release more than the stay. Do not treat when releasing your dog. If he gets up as you are reaching the treat toward him, pull it away and start the stay over.

Stage 2, the rest of the week: Begin to add distance into your stay work. At first just take a

28

tiny step back and return quickly to your dog (pretend you are on a bungee cord and pulled right back). If your dog gets up when you try to step back, begin by just swaying back a bit and quickly reward for the stay. Then move a bit more, and reward. Work up to taking a full step back, and when that is easy for your dog, begin to take two steps back, then when that is easy, three steps. Mix up how many steps you are taking once you get to three steps. Your goal for the week is to try to work up to six steps away from your dog, returning quickly.

DO NOT TURN YOUR BACK ON THE DOG AT THIS STAGE – if you break eye contact your dog will think you are done with the exercise and will almost certainly get up. We will work on breaking eye contact and walking away at a later stage. Do several stays in a row before releasing him. After each stay, go back to him, give him a treat (don't touch him or praise him), and calmly do another stay, repeating 3 or 4 times, then release and praise him.

NOTE: If your dog is well-trained in "Stay", begin to work on the "Relaxation Protocol". This is a systematic way to increase distractions with little effort on your part, by a series of progressive stays created by behaviorist Dr. Karen Overall, recorded courtesy of Roxanne Hawn, and you can download the MP3's at:

http://www.championofmyheart.com/relaxation
-protocol-mp3-files/

Although these exercises are called "days," they
are really "steps". Stay on "Day 1" until your dog
can do it without getting up during the exercise,
and then move to "Day 2", etc. I prefer to do these with the dog in a "Down" rather than a "Sit",
since it is a more relaxed position. After a bit, you
don't need to say "Stay" for each part. Quietly
give your dog a treat after each individual stay,
and release at the end of the session. If your dog
gets up, try to get him back into a down and continue on.

If he gets up each time you get to a certain point,
work on just that step separately before trying
the whole "Day" again. Remember – never reprimand the dog for a mistake, just help him do
better next time.

Each Day: Do "Nothing In Life Is Free" with
your dog.

Every single time your dog wants something,
wait for a sit. Don't ask for it, just wait until he
does it and then say, "Yes!" and give him what it
is that he is sitting for. Situations you should use
this for include:
- Putting his food bowl down
- Getting out of his crate or confined area

- Going outside
- Getting his leash on or off
- Getting a new chew bone
- Playing with a toy
- Snuggling with you
- Before he gets in or out of the car
- Before he can greet guests

This one exercise helps to build your dog's self-control and helps him see that he is not the one who makes the rules. All members of the family should do this simple thing. Very shortly your dog will figure out that sitting gets him what he wants, and he will begin to sit quickly anytime he wishes you to do something for him.

Soon he will figure that if he doesn't know what you want from him, sit might be a good idea. This is great for you, since when your dog is sitting, he's not jumping on you, begging, barking at you, etc. This is one of the most important things you can teach your dog, so be sure to do it.

If you want a terrific recall, it is especially important to get your dog to tune into you as the source of all good things, so be sure to do this for everything your dog wants.

Remember: Keep sessions short and fun!

END OF WEEK ONE CHECKLIST

Before you move ahead, can your dog:
- Sit on command and wait for a release before getting up?
- Lie down on command and wait for a release before getting up?
- Accept you touching his collar without flinching or pulling away?
- Respond quickly to simple recalls in the house with no distractions?
- Follow you around the house at your side for several minutes?
- Allow you to hold treats in your hand without lunging toward them?
- Stay in a sit or down until released for 5 seconds?
- Stay in a sit or down until released while you take a few steps back and return to him?

If the answer to any of the above is "No", please spend some more time on Week One before trying to move ahead. This work is progressive, and if your dog doesn't have a good understanding of Week One, he will not be able to do the exercises in next week's lesson yet. Take the time you need to build a strong foundation, and then moving ahead will become easy!

Week Two

Things to accomplish:

- Understand the importance of setting your dog up for success
- Work on "Sit" – work toward "snappy"
- Work on "Down" – work toward "snappy"
- Work on more recall exercises
- Practice leash walking with attention – "Let's Go!"
- Practice "Leave It" Stage Two
- Work on "Stay" with increasing distractions

Setting Your Dog Up For Success

One of the key parts of more advanced training is to balance the need to increase the difficulty of the exercise with your dog's ability to succeed at it. If you aimed at 100% success every try, you would be unable to move forward, since each time you add challenges, you increase the chance of a mistake on his part.

We will move forward with the 80/20 rule set out by master trainer Bob Bailey – if your dog can do an exercise 8 times out of 10, you can make it a bit more difficult. On the other hand, if he fails twice in a row, it's time to back up and make things easier for several tries before attempting the exercise where your dog made the error again.

To use a simple example of eye contact: You have worked with your dog on eye contact, and he can now maintain eye contact with you for 10 seconds at least 80% of the time. You now ask for 11 seconds. He fails. You again ask for 11 seconds. He fails again. You now begin working on easier durations, such as 6, 8, 5, 10, 8, 10, 9 and 7. If he is successful, you should then try for 11 seconds again.

Recalling guidelines for this week:

- Warm up with easy recalls before asking for more challenging ones.
- Practice in the house, at close distances the beginning of the week.
- When you try recalling outside, be sure that there are no major distractions around, such as cats, wildlife, other dogs, etc.
- Use medium to high level rewards for recalls.
- Slowly begin to add more distance.
- Collar grab so he won't take a treat and then run away – you want him to stay around you after he comes back. To this

end, treat more than one time for most re-calls.

- Once in a while, give him a "Fine Dining" experience – 30 full seconds of tiny bits of treats along with lots of affection and sweet talk.
- Remember to "cheerlead" him to you – no silences during the recall, just lots of cheering and saying "Good!".
- Keep your training sessions short and fun.
- Practice many times in order to build an automatic response and create "muscle memory".
- Don't repeat your cue ("Come", "Now", "Here" – whatever word you are using) if he doesn't come to you. Don't teach your dog to ignore you over and over. Either make yourself interesting enough that he will finally come to you, or go get him. Just be sure not to play "keep away", where he is almost letting you catch him and then run-ning away. Even if you have to throw yourself on the ground, be interesting!

THINGS TO DO THIS WEEK

Each Day: Practice the "Sit" exercise with a re-lease (Implied "Stay"). "C" value treats.

Continue asking your dog to "Sit" using the methods we used last week. As the week progresses, begin to wait longer before saying "Okay" and moving to release him. Begin to give treats only for faster than average sits. If he looks "snappy", give him a jackpot!

Each Day: Practice the "Down" exercise with a release (Implied "Stay"). "C" value treats.

Same as "Sit" only with a "Down" instead. You should work hard on getting a verbal cue in place (the word "Down" instead of a hand signal). If you are having trouble with this, try increasing your treats to "B" value instead of "C". If your dog does a "snappy" or fast down, reward him with a jackpot and lots of praise – this is what we are after.

Each Day: Practice simple recalls to improve your dog's focus on you. "B" value treats.

Be sure to warm up with a couple of simple recalls from last week's exercises first.
Exercise 1: Toy recall. When your dog is mildly distracted, grab one of his toys and run away, calling him while dangling his toy. When he arrives, have a great game of tug or throw the toy (no Collar Grab or treats for this game - the game is the reward).

Exercise 2: Toss a Treat and Run. Toss a treat in a corner near you, say "Get it!", and while your dog is eating it, run away and call him. When he arrives, CG (grab his collar) and treat. (Note: you are tossing the treat to get a head start!)

Exercise 3: Puppy Ping Pong. Call your dog back and forth between two or more people. Call him and when he arrives, CG and treat, then the next person calls. As he gets an understanding of this game, he will begin to head toward the next person without waiting to be called. This is great – call him anyway! If he won't leave a person, they must ignore the dog and look up while the person who called him makes noises and movements to get him to come. THEY MUST NOT CALL HIM MORE THAN ONCE!!!

Exercise 4: Hide and Seek. While someone holds the dog or distracts him, another person hides somewhere nearby, then calls the dog. When he finds them, have a puppy party! Be excited, tell him how smart he is, give him treats! As the week goes on, hide in harder places.

As the week progresses and your dog understands the games, play them in different locations both in the house and outside. Be sure to give him a "Fine Dining" experience at least once for every ten or so good responses.

Each Day: Work on "Let's Go". "B" value treats in house, "A" when outside.

"Let's Go" is a less formal version of "Heel". Heel means "stay exactly at my left leg, moving with me until I stop, then sit". "Let's Go" means walk with me on my left side, and it's your job to pay some attention to me and not pull on the leash. For all but tiny dogs, use a front clip harness for leash walking from now on. This exercise is just like the second part of Exercise 2 from last week, except that we are now using a leash.

In a quiet area inside, with your dog leashed, get your dog by your side in the "Reinforcement Zone", give him a treat or two, and say "Let's Go" and take a few steps. After a couple of steps, say "Yes!" and give him a great treat. Then take another couple of steps, and if he goes with you, say "Yes!" and give him a treat. This week, continue walking around with him, saying "Yes!" and giving him a treat, varying from two to ten steps.

Just walk around, treating every few steps, getting him used to being next to you, exactly like last week, except this time he is leashed. Vary your speed and direction so he has to pay attention to what you are doing. You can say "This way" when you change directions to help your pup go along with you. Just do this for a minute or two several times a day. Next week we will begin to make this more challenging.

IF HE PULLS: STOP! Do not let your dog pull you somewhere ever again! From now on, tension on the leash means he DOESN'T get where he's headed, instead of he does. Wait for him to look back at you (most likely he will be wondering why you aren't following him like you used to), and coax him back by your side (use kissy noises or pat your leg – do not call him), and when he's back in position, say "Let's Go" and take a step or two, and if he doesn't pull, say "Yes!" and give him a treat. Have patience with this – your dog has most likely learned to get somewhere by pulling you to it, and he has to learn that the rules have changed now, not to mention that he sees your pace as incredibly slow.

If you walk your dog on the leash outdoors during the week, even if you do nothing else with this, stop allowing him to pull. The instant the leash gets tight, you stop and wait until he loosens it before you get going again. Be sure to praise and/or treat for loosening up the leash, but don't give him treats until he has walked nicely for a few steps with you, or he will "yo-yo" out to the end of the leash and back to you for a treat. And don't use a retractable leash, or you will have no control over him at all.

Each Day: Increase the level of Impulse Control work. "C" value treats.

Leave It Stage 2: Your dog should be a champion at "Leave It" Stage 1, treats in your hand. You are now going to increase the challenge for him. With your dog sitting in front of you, say "Leave It" and place a small pile of low value treats on the floor in front of him. As he grabs for the treats, cover the pile with your hand quickly, being sure he does not get a treat. Let him sniff, lick, paw, nibble and even bite at your hand – don't move at all, don't say anything. Wait until he stops trying to get at the food out of frustration, then quickly remove your hand and give him another chance at it.

Go through the process again until he gives up, then remove your hand again. When he finally figures out that trying to take a treat won't get him one and he doesn't move at it, pick a treat up with your other hand and feed it to him. If he tries for the treats again, repeat the process.

Keep this up until you can feed him the treats one at a time without him trying to get them himself. Remember to only tell the dog to "Leave It" at the beginning. Praise each time you feed him, and release him when you are done.

Each Day: Work on "Sit-Stay" and "Down-Stay". "B" value treats inside, "A" when outside.

Remember the three factors in the "Stay" command – distance, duration and distractions. This week, begin to add mild distance and duration challenges to your dog's "Stay". Do this one at a time – while you work on longer stays, stick close to him. When you work on stays from farther away, don't ask for long stays. Remember to increase difficulty in small increments – the biggest mistake most owners make is trying to move too fast. This is an important exercise, so be sure to create a strong foundation.

If you find he breaks his stay, use a body block to keep him in place if you can. If not, just put him back in the same spot and start over. If he cannot hold the stay you are asking for, you are probably asking for too much. Make it a bit easier and try again. Remember to treat during the stay, and release with an "Okay". Don't make the release exciting – you don't want him to feel that being released is a big fun thing.

Begin to walk in different directions, and start walking around your dog (in small increments - remember to always work up to the full exercise). Start turning your back - at first just a quarter turn and right back, then a half-turn and right back, and then turn away from the dog and take one step and return, etc.

By the end of the week, try to have your dog able to stay in front of you in a sit or down for 20 seconds without getting up, and to be able to handle you walking 3 steps back, 3 steps to the right and 3 steps to the left.

NOTE: If your dog is doing well with "Stay", begin to work on the "Relaxation Protocol" (see Week One). If it turns out that he can't do the first day without getting up, go back and work on simple stays some more. You can download MP3's of these at:

http://www.championofmyheart.com/relaxation-protocol-mp3-files/

Although these exercises are called "days" they are really "steps". Stay on "Day 1" until your dog can do it without getting up during the exercise, and then move to "Day 2", etc. I prefer to do these with the dog in a "Down" rather than a "Sit", since it is a more relaxed position. After a bit, you don't need to say "Stay" for each part. Quietly give your dog a treat after each individual stay, and release at the end of the session. If your dog gets up, try to get him back into a down and continue on. If he gets up each time you get to a certain point, work on just that step separately before trying the whole "Day" again. Remember – never reprimand the dog for a mistake, just help him do better next time.

Each Day: Do "Nothing In Life Is Free" with your dog.

Every single time your dog wants something, wait for a sit. Don't ask for it, just wait until he does it and then say, "Yes!" and give him what it is that he is sitting for. Situations you should use this for include:

- Putting his food bowl down
- Getting out of his crate or confined area
- Going outside
- Getting his leash on or off
- Getting a new chew bone
- Playing with a toy
- Snuggling with you
- Before he gets in or out of the car
- Before he can greet guests

This one exercise helps to build your dog's self-control and helps him see that he is not the one who makes the rules. All members of the family should do this simple thing. Very shortly your dog will figure out that sitting gets him what he wants, and he will begin to sit quickly anytime he wishes you to do something for him. Soon he will figure that if he doesn't know what you want from him, sit might be a good idea. This is great for you, since when your dog is sitting, he's not jumping on you, begging, barking at you, etc. This is one of the most important things you can teach your dog, so be sure to do it.

If you want a terrific recall, it is especially important to get your dog to tune into you as the source of all good things, so be sure to do this for everything your dog wants.

Remember: Keep sessions short and fun!

END OF WEEK TWO CHECKLIST

Before you move ahead, can your dog:
- Sit on command quickly and easily and wait for a release before getting up?
- Lie down on command quickly and easily and wait for a release before getting up?
- Respond quickly to simple recalls outside with no distractions?
- Respond quickly to this week's recall exercises inside the house?
- Walk nicely on leash around the house at your side for several minutes?
- Allow you to put a pile of treats on the floor without lunging toward them?
- Stay in a sit or down until released for 20 seconds?
- Stay in a sit or down until released while you take 6 steps back and return to him? While you walk 3 steps to his left or right?

If the answer to any of the above is "No", please spend some more time on Week Two before trying to move ahead. This work is progressive, and if your dog doesn't have a good understanding of Week Two, he will not be able to do the exercises in next week's lesson yet. Take the time you need to build a strong foundation, and then moving ahead will become easy!

Week Three

Things to accomplish:

- Understand the importance of practice and testing your progress
- Keep working on "Sit" and "Down" to get fast, reflexive responses
- Work on "Down" – behind a barrier
- Work on more recall exercises
- Practice leash walking with attention – targeting
- Practice "Leave It" Stage Three
- Work on "Stay" – Relaxation Protocol

You Get Out Of It What You Put Into It

The true secret to a great recall is practice. You must be continually working on it, testing it and improving it, so that your dog becomes fluent at it. This process is similar to you learning any new skill. At first it is difficult – you have to think about each part of the process, and you are not especially good at it. As you practice more, it becomes easier for you, until eventually you become fluent – your body takes over and you no longer have to think about what to do, you just know.

Fluency is necessary for a great recall, because the only way your dog will come back to you in the presence of terrific distractions such as squirrels is that he no longer thinks about whether to obey – he just does it.

Although practice is the most important thing you can do to build fluency, don't overlook the need for testing your progress. If you do thousands of recalls in your kitchen, your dog will have a better recall, but since you haven't worked outside, he may still not be up to the challenges presented there. Testing stretches your dog's abilities.

The process must be in this order: build the behavior up, then test it. Don't test things you haven't trained. This would be like your teacher giving a final exam before the course started – backwards.

Testing provides you with valuable information. Whether your dog succeeds or fails, it tells you where you are in your training plan.

Recalling guidelines for this week:

- Warm up with easy recalls before asking for more challenging ones.
- Practice in the house, at close distances the beginning of the week.
- When you try recalling outside, be sure that there are no major distractions around, such as cats, wildlife, other dogs, etc.
- Use medium to high level rewards for recalls.
- Slowly begin to add more distance.
- Collar grab so he won't take a treat and then run away – you want him to stay around you after he comes back. To this end, treat more than one time for most recalls.
- Once in a while, give him a "Fine Dining" experience – 30 full seconds of tiny bits of treats along with lots of affection and sweet talk.
- Remember to "cheerlead" him to you – no silences during the recall, just lots of cheering and saying "Good!".
- Keep your training sessions short and fun.
- Practice many times in order to build an automatic response and create "muscle memory".
- Don't repeat your cue ("Come", "Now", "Here" – whatever word you are using) if he doesn't come to you. Don't teach your

dog to ignore you over and over. Either make yourself interesting enough that he will finally come to you, or go get him. Just be sure not to play "keep away", where he is almost letting you catch him and then running away. Even if you have to throw yourself on the ground, be interesting!

THINGS TO DO THIS WEEK

Each Day: Practice the "Sit" and "Down" exercises with a release (Implied "Stay"). "C" value treats.

Continue asking your dog to "Sit" using the methods we used last week. Give treats only for faster than average sits. If he looks "snappy", give him a jackpot! Also work on "Down" the same way, trying for "snappy" downs. We want to build a reflexive response to these commands.

Each Day: Practice the "Down" exercise behind a barrier. "B" value treats.

Put up a baby gate or similar barrier, and ask your dog to "Down" while he is on one side and you are on the other, with both of you near the gate. If he has trouble with this, use your hand signal ON YOUR SIDE OF THE GATE. As the week goes on, gradually begin to stand back a bit from the gate. If he does the "Down", go right to him and reward him. If not, move closer again for a bit before trying again. If your dog does a "snappy" or fast down, reward him with a jackpot and lots of praise – this is what we are after.

Each Day: Practice many types of recalls to improve your dog's focus. "A" value treats.

Be sure to warm up with a couple of simple recalls first.

Exercise 1: Restrained recall. Have a helper hold your dog. Stand a few feet away and start to rev him up by saying, "Ready, Ready, Ready....Puppy Come (your dog's name and cue)!" and run away. As soon as you call your dog, your helper should let him go so he can run to you. When he arrives, grab his collar and give him his treat with enthusiasm!

Exercise 2: Call Away. Have a helper talk to your dog. While your dog is watching your helper, call him enthusiastically. When he arrives, CG and treat. If he doesn't leave your helper, she should totally ignore the dog while you make noises and run away from him. If he still doesn't come, work on easier exercises a while longer before trying this again. Then try again with you and your helper closer together. DON'T CALL YOUR DOG MORE THAN ONCE!!!

Exercise 3: Toss & Call. Toss a low level treat away from you (large enough that your dog can find it, maybe a piece of carrot or apple). Give the dog a chance to eat the food, and then call him. When he arrives, give him a jackpot with something fantastic, like chicken or roast beef, or a great game of tug. Make sure your dog loves what you give him when he comes back much more than what you toss away.

Exercise 4: Setups with easy distractions from your list (1-3). Start working on having your dog come to you while around the easiest distractions from your list (Week One). Be sure to use your best treats as you begin to challenge him.

As the week progresses and your dog understands the games, play them in different locations both in the house and outside. Be sure to give him a "Fine Dining" experience at least once for every ten or so good responses.

Each Day: Work on "Let's Go". "B" value treats in house, "A" when outside.

Continue to work on "Let's Go", both inside and out. Begin to require more distance between treats. Pick spots as targets to walk to without a treat. Pick a spot a 5 feet away or so, and try to walk to it without using food, just your voice and movements to keep your dog paying attention to you. Be sure to talk to your dog so he can more easily focus on you. As he gets better at this, increase the distance between targets.

Make sure you keep walks interesting – change speed and direction often. Stop and ask for "Sits" and "Downs" and even short "Stays" while outside, remembering to keep it short and easy since you are in such a distracting environment.

Always have high value treats with you so that if your dog walks nicely when you didn't ask for it, or if he looks at you, you can reward him so that he'll do it more often.

Each Day: Increase the level of Impulse Control work. "C" value treats.

Leave It Game Stage Three: At this point, your dog should easily resist a handful of treats, and should be getting great at not charging at a pile of treats on the floor. Be sure to keep practicing these steps, but do it in different locations so your dog understands that it's not just something for the living room, but anywhere.

We will now "up the ante" by adding movement to the treats. This engages the dog's prey drive, and makes it a real challenge. You should now begin to drop treats near him, place them on his feet, roll them past him, etc. to clinch the lesson that when you say "Leave It", it doesn't matter what it is doing, the dog should not try to grab it. Begin to practice with toys or other objects that the dog is interested in. Make sure your dog can't grab the treat or object before you can protect it! Move the treat a bit farther away from the dog if necessary.

BE SURE TO ALWAYS SAY "GET IT!" WHENEVER ALLOWING YOUR DOG TO PICK SOMETHING UP FROM THE FLOOR OR THIS LESSON WILL NOT BE EFFECTIVE!!!

Each Day: Work on "Sit-Stay" and "Down-Stay". "B" value treats inside, "A" when outside.

If you haven't already done so, begin to work on the "Relaxation Protocol" (see Week One). You can download MP3's of these at:

http://www.championofmyheart.com/relaxation -protocol-mp3-files/

Although these exercises are called "days" they are really "steps". Stay on "Day 1" until your dog can do it without getting up during the exercise, and then move to "Day 2", etc. I prefer to do these with the dog in a "Down" rather than a "Sit", since it is a more relaxed position. After a bit, you don't need to say "Stay" for each part. Quietly give your dog a treat after each individual stay, and release at the end of the session. If your dog gets up, try to get him back into a down and continue on. If he gets up each time you get to a certain point, work on just that step separately before trying the whole "Day" again. Remember – never reprimand the dog for a mistake, just help him do better next time.

If you've already been working on the RP, continue to do so this week, moving to the next "Day" as your dog is ready.

Continue to work on simple stays outside, with your highest value treats. Add more challenges to these outdoor stays as your dog demonstrates that he is ready for them.

Each Day: Do "Nothing In Life Is Free" with your dog.

Every single time your dog wants something, wait for a sit. Don't ask for it, just wait until he does it and then say, "Yes!" and give him what it is that he is sitting for. Situations you should use this for include:

- Putting his food bowl down
- Getting out of his crate or confined area
- Going outside
- Getting his leash on or off
- Getting a new chew bone
- Playing with a toy
- Snuggling with you
- Before he gets in or out of the car
- Before he can greet guests

This one exercise helps to build your dog's self-control and helps him see that he is not the one who makes the rules. All members of the family should do this simple thing. Very shortly your dog will figure out that sitting gets him what he wants, and he will begin to sit quickly anytime he wishes you to do something for him. Soon he will figure that if he doesn't know what you want from him, sit might be a good idea. This is great for you, since when your dog is sitting, he's not jumping on you, begging, barking at you, etc. This is one of the most important things you can teach your dog, so be sure to do it.

If you want a terrific recall, it is especially important to get your dog to tune into you as the source of all good things, so be sure to do this for everything your dog wants.

Remember: Keep sessions short and fun!

END OF WEEK THREE CHECKLIST

Before you move ahead, can your dog:

- Sit on command quickly and easily and wait for a release before getting up?
- Lie down on command quickly and easily and wait for a release before getting up?
- Lie down behind a barrier when you ask from several feet away? And stay down until released?
- Respond quickly to all prior week's recall exercises outside?
- Respond quickly to this week's recall exercises inside the house?
- Walk nicely on leash outside at your side for several minutes while no distractions are nearby (i.e. other dogs, people, squirrels)?
- Allow you to drop or roll treats on the floor without lunging toward them?
- Successfully complete at least "Day One" of the Relaxation Protocol?

If the answer to any of the above is "No", please spend some more time on Week Three before trying to move ahead. This work is progressive, and if your dog doesn't have a good understanding of Week Three, he will not be able to do the exercises in next week's lesson yet. Take the time you need to build a strong foundation, and then moving ahead will become easy!

Week Four

Things to accomplish:

- Remember that failure doesn't mean anything except information
- Keep working on "Sit" and "Down" to get fast, reflexive responses
- Work on "Down" – from a distance
- Work on more recall exercises
- Practice leash walking with attention
- Practice "Leave It" Stage Four, on leash
- Work on "Stay" – Relaxation Protocol

What If He Doesn't Come When I Call Him?

When you are working with your dog, keep in mind that he is telling you how things are going by what his responses are. When he doesn't do what you expected, he's just giving you feedback – you haven't worked hard enough to get a reliable response for that exercise.

Remember how we discussed earlier that in the beginning, it should be extremely easy to succeed and extremely hard to fail. Now we are working in the middle stages of training – it's considerably easier to fail, but still not too hard to do it right. Any failures at this point just point out your weak spots – things you need to work on. Your dog is learning to ignore distractions in favor of coming to you, which is a really hard thing for him. Don't assume he can just do this – you must practice tenaciously if you want to see consistently great results – think of yourself learning any new skill. Nothing worthwhile happens overnight.

To review what we do when we hit an exercise that your dog can't do: back up and do easier versions of the exercise for a few sessions (or even days), until you feel there's a very good likelihood that he can do the harder version. Then test and see. If he can do it at least 80% of the time, great. Otherwise, make it easier again.

Keep in mind that a dog is not a machine, and like you, he will have good days and bad days. If he is distracted or uninterested in working, STOP. Ask for something really easy so that you end on a good response, and try again another time. There is no value in repeating mistakes or getting frustrated.

Recalling guidelines for this week:

- Warm up with easy recalls before asking for more challenging ones.
- Practice new exercises in the house, at close distances the beginning of the week. Easier exercises should be practiced outside as much as possible.
- When you try recalling outside, be sure that there are no major distractions around, such as cats, wildlife, other dogs, etc. unless you intend on working around them.
- Use medium (inside) to high (outside) level rewards for recalls.
- Slowly begin to add more distance.
- Collar grab so he won't take a treat and then run away – you want him to stay around you after he comes back. To this end, treat more than one time for most re-calls.
- Once in a while, give him a "Fine Dining" experience – 30 full seconds of tiny bits of treats along with lots of affection and sweet talk.
- Remember to "cheerlead" him to you – no silences during the recall, just lots of cheering and saying "Good!".
- Keep your training sessions short and fun.
- Practice many times in order to build an automatic response and create "muscle memory".

- Don't repeat your cue ("Come", "Now", "Here" – whatever word you are using) if he doesn't come to you. Don't teach your dog to ignore you over and over. Either make yourself interesting enough that he will finally come to you, or go get him. Just be sure not to play "keep away", where he is almost letting you catch him and then running away. Even if you have to throw yourself on the ground, be interesting!

THINGS TO DO THIS WEEK

Each Day: Practice the "Sit" and "Down" exercises with a release (Implied "Stay"). "C" value treats.

Continue asking your dog to "Sit" using the methods we used last week. Give treats only for faster than average sits. If he looks "snappy", give him a jackpot! Also work on "Down" the same way, trying for "snappy" downs. We want to build a reflexive response to these commands.

Each Day: Practice the "Down" Exercise from a distance. "B" value treats.

Put your dog in a sit-stay, move a few feet away from him, and ask your dog to "Down". If he does the down right where you left him, say "Yes!" and quickly return and give him a treat. If he moves toward you, you move toward him quickly saying "Down" again. As he begins to understand not to move toward you, begin to increase the distance.

Don't raise the challenges too fast, and if he can't do this at all after a few tries, go back to using the barrier for a few days before trying again. If your dog does a "snappy" or fast down, reward him with a jackpot and lots of praise – this is what we are after.

Each Day: Practice many types of recalls to improve your dog's focus. "A" value treats.

Be sure to warm up with a couple of simple recalls first.

Exercise 1: Toss & Call (out of reach). With your dog on leash, toss a low value treat away from you and well out of reach of your dog. As your dog begins to move toward the treat, call him back to you for a high value reward. Do this with toys as well. This is like last week's "Toss & Call" exercise, only harder, since you are not letting the dog get the tossed treat this time.

Exercise 2: Call Away (smelling food). Have a helper hold some low level food, and let your dog sniff it. Call him enthusiastically. When he arrives, CG and treat. If he doesn't leave your helper, she should remove the food and totally ignore the dog while you make noises and run away from him. If he still doesn't come, work on easier exercises a while longer before trying this again. Then try again with you and your helper closer together. DON'T CALL YOUR DOG MORE THAN ONCE!!! Make sure you have high level treats and your helper has low level ones.

Exercise 3: Smelly Food Recall. You need two helpers or one helper and your dog in a strong "Stay". Set your helper up on a chair in a hallway or other long path in your house, and have her hold a plastic container of smelly food, such as canned dog or cat food, liverwurst, tuna, etc.). Make sure they are a little away from the path the dog must run to come to you. With your dog restrained by a second helper (or in a "Stay") in one end of the hall and you at the other, call your dog past the food. If he goes to the food instead of you, the helper holding it must quickly put a lid on it. The next time, move the food farther away from the path and try again. If the dog fails again, work on easier exercises for a while before retrying. YOU MUST USE "A" VALUE TREATS AND DO "FINE DINING" IF YOUR DOG IGNORES THE SMELLY FOOD!!! This is a great success for him!!!

Exercise 4: Mix-It-Up Recalls. Begin to call him while you look different. Call while you are turned away from him, while you are in a chair, kneeling, lying on the floor on your back, on the floor on your stomach, while you are walking away from him, crawling away from him. Be sure to have fun and enjoy yourself with this, and your dog will love coming to you no matter what you're doing.

Exercise 5: Setups with medium distractions from your list (4-6). Start working on having your dog come to you while around harder distractions from your list (Week One). Be sure to use your best treats as you continue to challenge him.

As the week progresses and your dog understands the games, play them in different locations both in the house and outside. Be sure to give him a "Fine Dining" experience at least once for every ten or so good responses.

Each Day: Work on "Let's Go". "B" value treats in house, "A" when outside.

Continue to work on "Let's Go", both inside and out. Continue to require more distance between treats. Pick spots as targets to walk to without a treat like we did last week. Be sure to talk to your dog so he can more easily focus on you.

Make sure you keep walks interesting – change speed and direction often. Stop and ask for "Sits" and "Downs" and even short "Stays" while outside, remembering to keep it short and easy since you are in such a distracting environment.

Always have high value treats with you so that if your dog walks nicely when you didn't ask for it, or if he looks at you, you can reward him so that he'll do it more often.

Each Day: Increase the level of Impulse Control work. "B" value treats.

Leave It Game Stage Four: At this point, your dog should be easily dealing with Stages One and Two of "Leave It", in your hand and a pile on the floor. He should be able to resist food and toys moving near him, Stage Three. Now you should begin to use the "Leave It" command about other objects while on leash. Take leash walks in the house, with objects set up for you to walk past. As you approach the object, say "Leave It" and when your dog looks at you, say "Yes!" and hustle past the object, and then give him a great treat. Don't stay and let him stare at it after he has looked away.

If he stares/pulls and won't look at you, WAIT. Don't try to make him look at you with movements or sounds, just hold him firmly where he is. Eventually he will look away from the object in frustration - at THAT INSTANT you must say "Yes!" and move with him quickly away from the object and give him a treat. Next time walk past the object from a greater distance to make it easier for him to look away.

Practice this outside with anything your dog wants to pull you to. There are countless wonderful opportunities for "Leave It" outside, and the easier it is for your dog to turn away from distractions on leash, the more likely he will ignore them when you call him. Outside you should always be using "A" value treats.

Each Day: Work on "Sit-Stay" and "Down-Stay". "B" value treats inside, "A" when outside.

If you haven't already done so, begin to work on the "Relaxation Protocol" (see Week One). This is a systematic way to increase distractions with little effort on your part, by a series of progressive stays created by behaviorist Dr. Karen Overall. You can download MP3's of these at:

http://www.championofmyheart.com/relaxation -protocol-mp3-files/

Although these exercises are called "days" they are really "steps". Stay on "Day 1" until your dog can do it without getting up during the exercise, and then move to "Day 2", etc. I prefer to do these with the dog in a "Down" rather than a "Sit", since it is a more relaxed position. After a bit, you don't need to say "Stay" for each part. Quietly give your dog a treat after each individual stay, and release at the end of the session. If your dog gets up, try to get him back into a down and continue on. If he gets up each time you get to a certain point, work on just that step separately before trying the whole "Day" again. Remember – never reprimand the dog for a mistake, just help him do better next time.

If you've already been working on the RP, continue to do so this week, moving to the next "Day" as your dog is ready.

Continue to work on stays outside, with your highest value treats. Add more challenges to these outdoor stays as your dog demonstrates that he is ready for them.

Each Day: Do "Nothing In Life Is Free" with your dog.

Every single time your dog wants something, wait for a sit. Don't ask for it, just wait until he does it and then say, "Yes!" and give him what it is that he is sitting for. Situations you should use this for include:

- Putting his food bowl down
- Getting out of his crate or confined area
- Going outside
- Getting his leash on or off
- Getting a new chew bone
- Playing with a toy
- Snuggling with you
- Before he gets in or out of the car
- Before he can greet guests

This one exercise helps to build your dog's self-control and helps him see that he is not the one who makes the rules. All members of the family should do this simple thing. Very shortly your dog will figure out that sitting gets him what he wants, and he will begin to sit quickly anytime he wishes you to do something for him. Soon he will figure that if he doesn't know what you want from him, sit might be a good idea. This is great for you, since when your dog is sitting, he's not jumping on you, begging, barking at you, etc. This is one of the most important things you can teach your dog, so be sure to do it.

If you want a terrific recall, it is especially important to get your dog to tune into you as the source of all good things, so be sure to do this for everything your dog wants.

Remember: Keep sessions short and fun!

END OF WEEK FOUR CHECKLIST

Before you move ahead, can your dog:
- Sit on command quickly and easily and wait for a release before getting up?
- Lie down on command quickly and easily and wait for a release before getting up?
- Lie down from a sit when you ask from several feet away without a barrier? And stay down until released?
- Respond quickly to all prior week's recall exercises outside?
- Respond quickly to this week's recall exercises inside the house?
- Walk nicely on leash outside at your side for at least 10 minutes while no distractions are nearby (i.e. other dogs, people, squirrels)?
- Walk past distractions in the house without lunging toward them?
- Successfully complete at least "Day Three" of the Relaxation Protocol?

If the answer to any of the above is "No", please spend some more time on Week Four before trying to move ahead. This work is progressive, and if your dog doesn't have a good understanding of Week Four, he will not be able to do the exercises in next week's lesson yet. Take the time you need to build a strong foundation, and then moving ahead will become easy!

Week Five

Things to accomplish:

- Remember to work at your dog's own pace
- Keep working on "Sit" and "Down" to get fast, reflexive responses
- Work on "Emergency Down" – "Down" when moving
- Work on more recall exercises
- Practice leash walking with attention
- Practice "Leave It" Stage Five, on and off leash
- Work on "Stay" – Relaxation Protocol

Don't Rush – Build that Foundation

One of the hardest things for most dog owners is holding back their enthusiasm to try harder exercises. There seems to be a human weakness for instant gratification, which is totally counterproductive when working on building a new skill.

When you begin training your dog, you are naturally excited about seeing his skills grow. But if you move too fast, his understanding of the job is weak. For recalls, this means he thinks, "Sometimes I come when I'm called, and sometimes I don't", because that's what he does when you move too fast. To get a reliable recall, he needs to believe that when you call, he comes. Period.

You get this response from him by following the basic guidelines for training a behavior:

- Train the early stages very well so that he has a full understanding of what you want from him (NOT "Sometimes I do it and sometimes I don't") – make it so easy he almost can't not do it and reward the heck out of good responses.
- Practice continually so that it becomes automatic for him to respond.
- Build up his ability to perform under more difficult circumstances gradually.
- Test his abilities and improve on the weak areas.
- Keep reinforcing great work throughout his life.

If your dog is not quite ready for an exercise in your lesson, it is far more important to strengthen the easier ones more than it is to push ahead where he will make mistakes. Build a strong foundation, however long it takes, and harder exercises will become easy.

Recalling guidelines for this week:

- Warm up with easy recalls before asking for more challenging ones.
- Practice new exercises in the house, at close distances the beginning of the week. Easier exercises should be practiced outside as much as possible.
- When you try recalling outside, be sure that there are no major distractions around, such as cats, wildlife, other dogs, etc. unless you intend on working around them.
- Use medium (inside) to high (outside) level rewards for recalls.
- Slowly begin to add more distance.
- Collar grab so he won't take a treat and then run away – you want him to stay around you after he comes back. To this end, treat more than one time for most recalls.
- Once in a while, give him a "Fine Dining" experience – 30 full seconds of tiny bits of treats along with lots of affection and sweet talk.
- Remember to "cheerlead" him to you – no silences during the recall, just lots of cheering and saying "Good!".
- Keep your training sessions short and fun.
- Practice many times in order to build an automatic response and create "muscle memory".

- Don't repeat your cue ("Come", "Now", "Here" – whatever word you are using) if he doesn't come to you. Don't teach your dog to ignore you over and over. Either make yourself interesting enough that he will finally come to you, or go get him. Just be sure not to play "keep away", where he is almost letting you catch him and then running away. Even if you have to throw yourself on the ground, be interesting!

THINGS TO DO THIS WEEK

Each Day: Practice the "Sit" and "Down" exercises with a release (Implied "Stay"). "C" value treats.

Continue asking your dog to "Sit" using the methods we used last week. Give treats only for faster than average sits. If he looks "snappy", give him a jackpot! Also work on "Down" the same way, trying for "snappy" downs. We want to build a reflexive response to these commands.

Each Day: Practice the "Emergency Down" while moving. "B" value treats.

Wait until your dog is just wandering around, and "down" him while he's walking. He may respond slowly at first if he's not quite sure of what you want, but if he should figure it out pretty fast. When walking on leash, once in a while ask for a "Down" as you stop, instead of an automatic sit. Then you can start encouraging him to chase you (don't run very fast until he understands the what you're doing); as he catches up to you, turn to him and give the "Down" cue. Reward with a big jump-up release followed by treats and/or another chase game depending on what your dog likes best.

Begin using a large downward swoop of your arm as your "drop" signal while you are saying the word "Down". Make this fun for you and your dog!

Each Day: Practice many types of recalls to improve your dog's focus. "A" value treats.

Be sure to warm up with a couple of simple recalls first.

Exercise 1: Toss & Call (within reach). With your dog on leash, toss a low value treat away from you within of reach of your dog. As your dog begins to move toward the treat, call him back to you for a high value reward. Do this with toys as well. This is like last week's "Toss & Call" exercise, only harder, since you are tossing the treat within range this time. If he goes for the treat, go back to last week's exercise and work on getting the treat closer more gradually. Always have a much better treat as a reward.

Exercise 2: Call Away (eating food). Have a helper hold some low level food and let your dog nibble at it. Call him enthusiastically. When he arrives, CG and treat. If he doesn't leave your helper, she should remove the food and totally ignore the dog while you make noises and run away from him. If he still doesn't come, work on easier exercises a while longer before trying this again. Then try again with you and your helper closer together. DON'T CALL YOUR DOG MORE THAN ONCE!!! Make sure you have high level treats and your helper has low level ones.

Exercise 3: Mix-It-Up Recalls. Keep calling him while you look different. Call while you are turned away from him, while you are in a chair, kneeling, lying on the floor on your back, on the floor on your stomach, while you are walking away from him, crawling away from him. Be sure to have fun and enjoy yourself with this, and your dog will love coming to you no matter what you're doing.

Exercise 4: Food Bowl Recall. Have a helper hold your dog, or put him in a stay at the end of a hallway or area where you have a path he can run down. Take his food bowl and place it on the floor so that when you call him he will have to run past the bowl. Make a big show of putting some dry food in his bowl, and then quickly scoop it up in your hand so that the bowl is now empty again. Hide the food, go to your spot at the end of the hall, and call your dog. If he stops at the bowl, surprise! There isn't any food there! Set him up again and redo the recall, moving the bowl a bit farther off the path. If your dog fails twice in a row at this, work on easier recalls for a while before trying again. Be sure the food you will reward him with is his favorite, and the food you pretend to put in the bowl doesn't matter much to him. As he gets better at this, you can use better food when you pretend to put it in the bowl.

Exercise 5: Setups with medium/high distractions from your list (4-8). Start working on having your dog come to you while around harder distractions from your list (Week One). Be sure to use your best treats as you continue to challenge him. Remember not to challenge him with situations you know he's not ready for yet.

As the week progresses and your dog understands the games, play them in different locations both in the house and outside. Be sure to give him a "Fine Dining" experience at least once for every ten or so good responses.

Each Day: Work on "Let's Go". "B" value treats in house, "A" when outside.

Continue to work on "Let's Go", both inside and out. Continue to require more distance between treats. Pick spots as targets to walk to without a treat like we did last lesson. Be sure to talk to your dog so he can more easily focus on you.

Make sure you keep walks interesting – change speed and direction often. Stop and ask for "Sits" and "Downs" and even short "Stays" while outside, remembering to keep it short and easy since you are in such a distracting environment.

Always have high value treats with you so that if your dog walks nicely when you didn't ask for it, or if he looks at you, you can reward him so that he'll do it more often.

Each Day: Increase the level of Impulse Control work. "B" value treats.

Leave It Game Stage Five: Begin to set up difficult challenges for your dog, as he is ready. Plates of food on low tables, stuffed animals, chew toys. Once he doesn't even move toward the object at all when told to "Leave It", try working indoors off leash. Be sure to have a helper near who can prevent the dog from taking the object if he tries.

Each Day: Work on "Sit-Stay" and "Down-Stay". "B" value treats inside, "A" when outside.

If you haven't already done so, begin to work on the "Relaxation Protocol" (see Week One). You can download MP3's of these at:

http://www.championofmyheart.com/relaxation -protocol-mp3-files/

Although these exercises are called "days", they are really "steps". Stay on "Day 1" until your dog can do it without getting up during the exercise, and then move to "Day 2", etc. I prefer to do these with the dog in a "Down" rather than a "Sit", since it is a more relaxed position. After a bit, you don't need to say "Stay" for each part. Quietly give your dog a treat after each individual stay, and release at the end of the session.

If your dog gets up, try to get him back into a down and continue on. If he gets up each time you get to a certain point, work on just that step separately before trying the whole "Day" again. Remember – never reprimand the dog for a mistake, just help him do better next time.

If you've already been working on the RP, continue to do so this week, moving to the next "Day" as your dog is ready.

Continue to work on stays outside, with your highest value treats. Add more challenges to these outdoor stays as your dog demonstrates that he is ready for them.

Each Day: Do "Nothing In Life Is Free" with your dog.

Every single time your dog wants something, wait for a sit. Don't ask for it, just wait until he does it and then say, "Yes!" and give him what it is that he is sitting for. Situations you should use this for include:
- Putting his food bowl down
- Getting out of his crate or confined area
- Going outside
- Getting his leash on or off
- Getting a new chew bone
- Playing with a toy
- Snuggling with you
- Before he gets in or out of the car
- Before he can greet guests

This one exercise helps to build your dog's self-control and helps him see that he is not the one who makes the rules. All members of the family should do this simple thing. Very shortly your dog will figure out that sitting gets him what he wants, and he will begin to sit quickly anytime he wishes you to do something for him. Soon he will figure that if he doesn't know what you want from him, sit might be a good idea. This is great for you, since when your dog is sitting, he's not jumping on you, begging, barking at you, etc. This is one of the most important things you can teach your dog, so be sure to do it.

If you want a terrific recall, it is especially important to get your dog to tune into you as the source of all good things, so be sure to do this for everything your dog wants.

Remember: Keep sessions short and fun!

END OF WEEK FIVE CHECKLIST

Before you move ahead, can your dog:
- Sit on command quickly and easily and wait for a release before getting up?
- Lie down on command quickly and easily and wait for a release before getting up?
- Lie down quickly while moving around? And stay down until released?
- Respond quickly to all prior week's recall exercises outside?
- Respond quickly to this week's recall exercises inside the house?
- Walk nicely on leash outside at your side for at least 10 minutes while some low to medium level distractions from your list are in the distance?
- Leave things on command in the house without a leash on?
- Successfully complete at least "Day Five" of the Relaxation Protocol?

If the answer to any of the above is "No", please spend some more time on Week Five before trying to move ahead. This work is progressive, and if your dog doesn't have a good understanding of Week Five, he will not be able to do the exercises in next week's lesson yet. Take the time you need to build a strong foundation, and then moving ahead will become easy!

Week Six and Going Forward

Things to accomplish:

- Remember: Proofing: Use it or lose it
- Keep working on "Sit" and "Down" to get fast, reflexive responses
- Work on "Emergency Down" – during recalls
- Work on more recall challenges
- Practice leash walking with attention
- Practice "Leave It" in real life situations
- Work on "Stay" – Relaxation Protocol

Always Be Proofing – Use It or Lose It
Remember what we said last week about building a strong foundation. If it takes longer than six weeks to reach this point, that's fine. It's not about speed, it's about getting excellent, reliable responses.

It may turn out that your dog will never have a totally reliable recall. For some dogs, that's just not possible. Dogs that are hyper-sensitive to their environment, dogs that have been bred to follow their noses, dogs that relish running like the wind – these offer the biggest challenges to a trainer. And you are a trainer if you are working with your dog.

If you put your whole heart into building a great recall, even those dogs can learn to come when you call them almost all of the time, but may not be totally safe off leash. But you will have greatly improved the likelihood of them coming when it matters, so don't give up! This can save your dog's life.

From now on, you need to keep working on great responses. Maybe you aren't as far along as you hoped, or maybe your dog is doing really well. Either way, keep working on it. Once you're happy with your dog's recall and emergency down, you don't have to practice as much, but you do need to call your dog many times a week to keep him sharp. There are many opportunities during a day for a quick recall, so be sure to take some of them – and be sure to reward your dog for coming. And every week or so, test him on some of his challenges. You've worked this hard to get him doing well – don't let it slip away!

THINGS TO DO FROM NOW ON

Exercise: Practice the "Sit" and "Down" exercises with a release (Implied "Stay"). "C" value treats.

Continue asking your dog to "Sit" using the methods we used last week. Give treats only for faster than average sits. If he looks "snappy", give him a jackpot! Also work on "Down" the same way, trying for "snappy" downs. We want to build and maintain a reflexive response to these commands.

Exercise: Practice the "Emergency Down" or "Drop on Recall". "B" value treats.

Once your dog is great at dropping while moving, it's time to try to get him to drop while he's coming to you. Set this up in a non-distracting environment. Put your dog in a stay. Move about 10 feet away from your dog and call him. When he is about 3 feet from you, do your hand signal and say "Down!". If you have been working on your drops while moving, he should at least hesitate and start going down. Even if he takes an extra step or two toward you, reward him and enthusiastically release him from the down.

Gradually increase the distance from you when you give the "Down" cue and signal. Go to him for his reward/release in the early days of training this. As he improves, begin to hold his stay before going to him to release him. You need him not just to drop, but to freeze in place until you release him, if this is to be a safety cue.

Do not ask for a drop every time you call your dog, or you will slow his recall down. Aside from training sessions where you are specifically working on this, don't ask for a down more than once or twice for every ten recalls.

I can't stress enough how important this exercise is. Imagine your dog across the street, and he decides to come back to you when a car is coming. The "Emergency Down" will freeze him in place until it is safe for him to move. But you must practice this for the rest of his life, along with your recalls, in order for it to work when you need it.

Exercise: Practice many types of recalls to improve your dog's focus. "A" value treats.

Be sure to warm up with a couple of simple recalls first.

Recalls on a long line outside of a dog park. If possible, find a dog park with a field next to it, and practice various recalls and drops with the distraction of other dogs running, barking and playing nearby.

Recalls in new locations. Take your dog to parks, fields, empty parking lots – anywhere where there is space to work, and practice recalls and drops on a long line.

Recalls around people and dogs. Have other people running around while you work with your dog. If you know people with friendly dogs, have a playdate in a safe fenced area, and call your dog away from play periodically, then send him back to play. If your dog goes to a dog park, work there. Remember not to call him if you are sure he won't come back – work on his skills more first.

Setups with high distractions from your list (8-10). Start working on having your dog come to you while around the hardest distractions from your list (Week One) IF HE IS READY. Be sure to use your best treats as you continue to challenge him. Remember not to challenge him with situations you know he's not ready for yet.

As the week progresses and your dog understands the games, play them in different locations both in the house and outside. Be sure to give him a "Fine Dining" experience at least once for every ten or so good responses.

Exercise: Practice good leash walking – keep your dog's attention. "A" value treats.

From now on, require polite leash manners – no pulling, stay on your side, walk as if you are two friends taking a walk, side by side. The better your dog is at ignoring distractions on a walk, the stronger your recall will be.

Exercise: Use "Leave It" in real life situations regularly. "B" value treats.

Leave It Game Stage Six: Practice "Leave It" routinely on walks or in the house. Drop something from the counter, put out a booby trap for him, use it when you see a person walking by outside, or another dog. A strong "Leave It" helps with a strong recall.

Exercise: Work on "Sit-Stay" and "Down-Stay". "B" value treats inside, "A" when outside.
Keep working on the Relaxation Protocol, moving to the next "Day" as your dog is ready. If you complete the series, move to a different location and start again. Or, if you prefer, pick a random "Day" to practice.

Continue to work on stays outside, with your highest value treats. Add more challenges to these outdoor stays as your dog demonstrates that he is ready for them. Think about the things you have worked on in the Relaxation Protocol. Design similar challenges for your dog where you aren't listening to the mp3.

Exercise: Do "Nothing In Life Is Free" with your dog.

Every single time your dog wants something, wait for a sit. Don't ask for it, just wait until he does it and then say, "Yes!" and give him what it is that he is sitting for. Situations you should use this for include:
- Putting his food bowl down
- Getting out of his crate or confined area
- Going outside
- Getting his leash on or off
- Getting a new chew bone
- Playing with a toy
- Snuggling with you
- Before he gets in or out of the car
- Before he can greet guests

This one exercise helps to build your dog's self-control and helps him see that he is not the one who makes the rules. All members of the family should do this simple thing. Very shortly your dog will figure out that sitting gets him what he wants, and he will begin to sit quickly anytime he wishes you to do something for him. Soon he will figure that if he doesn't know what you want from him, sit might be a good idea. This is great for you, since when your dog is sitting, he's not jumping on you, begging, barking at you, etc. This is one of the most important things you can teach your dog, so be sure to do it.

If you want a terrific recall, it is especially important to get your dog to tune into you as the source of all good things, so be sure to do this for everything your dog wants.

Remember: Keep sessions short and fun!

END OF WEEK SIX CHECKLIST

Before you consider your dog at maintenance level, can your dog:

- Sit on command quickly and easily and wait for a release before getting up?
- Lie down on command quickly and easily and wait for a release before getting up?
- Lie down immediately when you tell him? Even if he is running to you? And stay down until released?
- Respond quickly to all prior week's recall exercises outside around distractions?
- Respond quickly to this week's recall exercises?
- Walk nicely on leash outside at your side for at least 20 minutes while occasionally a medium level distraction from your list is nearby? Walk past high level distractions without lunging toward them?
- Leave things on command outside in an enclosed area without a leash on?
- Successfully complete at least "Day Fifteen" of the Relaxation Protocol?

If the answer to any of the above is "No", please spend some more time on Week Six before considering the job done. And keep in mind the "Use It or Lose It" aspect to dog training. Just like playing a musical instrument, the secret to great performance is practice.

Once you feel that you have tested your dog successfully on all of the highest level situations you can think of, you can switch to "Maintenance". This simply means that you will keep asking your dog for this level of performance from now on – for all of the Week Six exercises. Several times a day you should call your dog when he's not expecting it, and several times each week practice his "Emergency Down". At least once a week, test him on his highest level distractions, and give him a "Fine Dining" experience at least once a week.

Remember not to ask for an "Emergency Down" each time you call him, or he will slow down while returning to you, expecting to lie down. Try to keep it to ten recalls for every one with a down.

Congratulations! You have reached a level of excellence that very few dog owners achieve! Give both you and your dog a big reward!

A NOTE ABOUT REWARDS

I feel very strongly that a good job deserves a reward. If you continue to reward your dog for excellence, he will be far more likely to continue to show it. Rewards don't need to be chicken and steak forever. As you practice this, the joy you show in his performance will be a reward to him as well.

Make sure you have a "Fine Dining" experience here and there, as well as play games or throw a ball – whatever your dog loves. Just don't take a great recall for granted, or it will go away.

Once in a while, imagine that when he ran to you, it just saved his life. Show him how you feel about that. He'll be glad you did – and he'll be more likely to come next time you call!

Appendix A – Benefits of Record Keeping

Keeping track of your training sessions has many benefits: you have a clear record of your progress, so if you are feeling like you're getting nowhere, you can go back and see just how far you have actually come; you can spot specific trouble areas that you may not have noticed before; you can make sure that you work consistently with your dog; and you can easily chart the path from where you are to where you want to be.

Most people don't keep good records, but if you do, you'll find your training efforts will pay off more quickly, since they will help so much with consistency in both what you are doing and how often you are doing it. I urge you to give it a try – for each session note the date, what you are working on, how many trials you did, what went right, what went wrong, and what is your plan for next time. Then the next time, quickly look over this sheet to see what you wanted to do as your starting point for that session. You'll be amazed at the progress you can make this way.

Appendix B – Glossary

CG – Collar Grab. See Week One.

Choice-Based Training: Training which encourages the dog to make decisions for himself. At first, the choices are limited to where making the "right" choice (the one you want him to make) is extremely easy. This helps him to quickly understand what he should do. As he builds his understanding, the choices become more challenging – distractions and temptations are added. If you don't move too fast, your dog gradually will become able to make the right decision in any circumstance.

Distractions: Things that may make your dog lose focus or decide not to obey you. When first teaching any behavior, you should make sure there are no distractions around. This includes other people, noises, interesting smells, toys nearby, commotion in the vicinity, etc. Once your dog is reliably obeying without distractions, then you begin "proofing", or carefully adding distractions to teach your dog that he can still listen when something else is around.

Fine Dining: An experience named by Leslie Nelson where you feed and praise and pet your dog for a full 30 seconds. Use wonderful food, and just pinch a bit at a time, and tell your dog how wonderful he is while he's nibbling his fabulous treats. Make this a super memorable experience, and try to do it at least once for every 10 recalls.

Jackpot: A special reward of 3 to 4 treats giving quickly one after another, in order to let your dog know that he has done something great! Times to use this would include the first time he does something correctly, when he has ignored a particularly difficult distraction, or just to surprise him and keep it fun.

Long Line: A very long leash or light rope attached to your dog, 20-50 feet long. If your dog is likely to run away, you should hold onto the other end (be careful not to get tangled up in it). If he doesn't run fast, or isn't likely to run off, then you can let the line drag on the ground – just be sure to grab it or step on it if your dog takes off. Use this to have a way to keep your dog safe when not indoors or in a fenced area.

Positive Reinforcement Training: Training which uses the scientific laws of learning by focusing on rewarding behaviors that you like and want to see again, and by ignoring or replacing behaviors that you don't like and want to eliminate. By using treats, games, and "real life" rewards we can influence how a dog behaves, and build new habits.

Proofing: The process of systematically working with your dog through more and more difficult distractions in order to be sure he can respond correctly no matter what is going on around him. Proofing should be done by carefully adding one distraction at a time, and working with that until your dog is able to ignore it, then moving on. Eventually you should be training around multiple distractions at the same time, but you must work up to this, or your dog will not be able to succeed.

Reinforcer: Rewards, such as food, games, going outside, getting in a car, taking a walk, belly rubs – anything a dog likes enough to be willing to do things for. Also called a motivator. Be sure the dog likes it – it's not a reinforcer if he doesn't care about it, even if you think it should be.

Reward: Reinforcer.

Setting the Dog Up For Success: When training, be sure that you don't move too fast for your dog, or he won't be able to be correct. When this happens often, he isn't getting enough feedback to know what you actually want from him, since you can't reward him, and you run the risk of getting frustrated. Step back and make it easier until he can reliably be correct, and then make the situation just a bit harder for him. If he can't focus on training, ask for something really easy, reward him, and stop for the time being. If you feel yourself getting frustrated, back up, get a good response to reward, and stop. Training should be fun for both of you – if it's not that day, just stop and try later.

Claim Your Free Bonus

FREE BONUS! Be sure to go to

http://www.ReallySimpleDogTraining.com/RTBonus.html

to get your FREE printable quick reference guide. This lets you print any or all of the lessons so that you don't have to refer to your book while training. Also be sure to print out your worksheets from Week One.

About the Author

Carol Miller is a Certified Dog Trainer, and an honors graduate of the Animal Behavior College. In addition to her series of dog training books (Really Simple Dog Training), she has written several children's books about nature and the world we live in.

She lives in New Jersey with her family, which includes two rescued Border Collies and 3 rescued cats.

Learn more about "Really Simple Dog Training" at

www.ReallySimpleDogTraining.com

48976570R00058

Made in the USA
San Bernardino, CA
09 May 2017